What do you know about animals?

How many questions can you answer?
It's fun to peek behind
the flap — to see if you
were right . . .

PRICE/STERN/SLOAN
Publishers, Inc., Los Angeles

What tall animal could reach right up there?

How many arms does an octopus have?

Where does Mrs. Kangaroo carry her young?

What's big, white and furry, and lives in the Arctic?

Why do camels have humps?

Do crocodiles lay eggs?

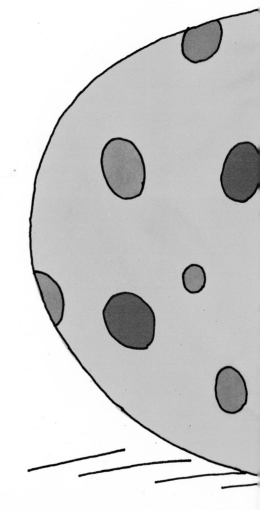

What dangerous snake has a rattle?

Can an ostrich fly?

What horse lives in the sea?